THE SPIRIT OF
CONTRADICTION

Borgo Press Books by CHARLES DUFRESNY

The Spirit of Contradiction & The Double Widowing: Two Plays
Straight from the Convent and Other Plays
The Village Coquette & The Crazy Wager: Two Plays

THE SPIRIT OF CONTRADICTION

& THE DOUBLE WIDOWING: TWO PLAYS

CHARLES DUFRESNY

Translated and Adapted by Frank J. Morlock

THE BORGO PRESS
MMXIII

THE SPIRIT OF CONTRADICTION

Copyright © 1986, 2013 by Frank J. Morlock

FIRST EDITION

Published by Wildside Press LLC

www.wildsidebooks.com

DEDICATION

For My Daughter, Michelle

CONTENTS

THE SPIRIT OF CONTRADICTION 9
CAST OF CHARACTERS. 10
THE PLAY 11
THE DOUBLE WIDOWING 73
CAST OF CHARACTERS. 74
ACT I 75
ACT II 109
ACT III 150
ABOUT THE TRANSLATOR. 169

THE SPIRIT OF CONTRADICTION

CAST OF CHARACTERS

Mr. Townly

Mrs. Townly

Lucas, the gardener

Angelica

Edward Richly

Mr. Nelson

Lawyer

Lackey

Six men, two women

THE PLAY

The scene is a garden before Mr. Townly's house in London. Lucas, the gardener, enters in a rage.

Lucas:

To hell with that bitch and her contradictory nature!

Townly:

There, there, Lucas, softly.

Lucas:

No, sir. I can no longer put up with your wife's temperament.

Townly:

You have to forgive her, because the spirit of contradiction is natural to her.

Lucas:

When she contradicts you like crazy—you, her

husband—that's natural, huh? Well, maybe. But it isn't natural that she should contradict my garden.

Townly:

Patience, Lucas, patience.

Lucas:

To be perfectly frank, I don't like being gardener here—or anywhere there are women. A woman in a garden causes more damage than a million hedgehogs.

Townly:

You're right and my wife is in the wrong.

Lucas:

Everything I've planted is torn up. She's replanted all the weeds I tore out when I was grafting. She said they're wildflowers. Then when I planted the cabbages, she said she now wants lettuces. Nothing is done by her order that doesn't reverse something I've done. Yesterday she half buried my prunes under melons. I believe—God pardon me!—that it would be better for me to plant watermelons in the grape arbor.

Townly:

She's unreasonable, but let's forget about that, Lucas. Let's talk about marrying my daughter. I need your advice about that matter.

Lucas:

I haven't got an idea in my head, because I've been fighting with Madam. That puts me in an uncultivated state—me and my garden. And besides, she's just discharged me.

Townly:

Don't worry about it. Never mind. I'll take care of you.

Lucas:

How are you going to take care of me against her—when you can't take care of yourself? Hey! Did I ever tell you that you're too easy with her? As soon as she says yes or no, you say the same.

Townly:

What do you want, Lucas? I love my wife. She has no other pleasure than to do exactly the opposite of what I want. So I provide her with that small satisfaction.

Lucas:

You do that if that's what you like. But don't worry, her humor is too settled for it to give her any satisfaction. So much for that, sir. As to your daughter, I'll be what help I can—but what do you intend to do?

Townly:

Well, you see, I've got to get my wife to agree—

Lucas:

Well, it's not up to me. I've tried to revive your spirit, but you won't do anything against her.

Townly:

Look, you've more imagination than I do. And more sense than philosophers—who haven't any, really.

Lucas:

Wait, sir. There are peasants who are sharp about acquiring money—but my philosophy is to govern the world like a careful gardener. You, for example, want to marry your daughter, but you don't know to whom. But me, I've seen it all in my garden. As I tell Madam, trees benefit from the sun, plants from the shade. So you see, if your daughter is ready to benefit from marriage, your wife will put her in a convent.

Townly:

You've said it exactly. If my daughter wishes to get married, she'd better not show it.

Lucas:

Madam has already tried to worm it out of me. "But Lucas," she said to me, "what do you think of this marriage?" "I think nothing, Madam." "But my daughter, for her part—" "Nothing." "But my husband, for his part—" Silence. "And because they know I can't breathe when I'm contradicted, they hide it from me. But it won't work. And I have tricks for figuring out when I'm being contradicted. It's a blind alley." What a woman. Very well. Leave it to me to put everything right. She's coming.

Townly:

I will wait for you in the arbor.

(Exit Townly)

Lucas:

I'd be very much put out to leave the employ of that bourgeois. His bourgeois money shines forth more splendidly than the money of noblemen who have a great deal more.

Mrs. Townly: (entering)

Have you just put yourself under the protection of my husband? He can tell me to keep you, but I am not going to obey him. Come quickly, give me the keys, and then I will give you your wages.

Lucas: (in a whining tone)

I am very upset about losing my situation with you.

(Then roaring)

Ha! Ha! Ha!

Mrs. Townly:

You are laughing, eh?

Lucas: (crying)

It overwhelms me.

(Roaring)

Ha, ha, ha!

Mrs. Townly:

What are you getting at?

Lucas:

Nothing, nothing, ha, ha, ha.

(Sadly)

Here, Madam, I am giving you the keys.

Mrs. Townly:

I know why you're laughing.

Lucas:

Ha, ha, ha, ha. I can't hold myself in. How nice to be thrown out. I'm not afraid of you. Ha, ha. I laugh like a merry-go-round at what you have done. Ha, ha, ha. Quite frankly, this is something that I expected for a long time from your difficult temperament, and I hope you are inexorable. I have said to myself, if Madam sees that I want to take my leave, she won't hear of it. If I ask for my wages, she'll let me fish for them rather than be of my opinion. Oh, it's much better if I anger her so she will throw me out.

Mrs. Townly:

What! Who says I'm throwing you out?

Lucas:

I have quarreled with you, ha, ha, ha. I'm giving you back your keys willingly enough.

Mrs. Townly:

Oh, I see. To get even you have decided to leave me without a gardener.

Lucas:

That's precisely what I'm going to do.

Mrs. Townly:

You can go when I have another.

Lucas:

You can have three right away.

Mrs. Townly:

Stay at least until tomorrow.

Lucas:

Tomorrow you'll no longer be in the mood to throw me out. I want to quit today.

Mrs. Townly:

No! It won't be said that I am your dupe. You wish to leave me and I do not wish you to leave.

Lucas:

One cannot keep people against their will. And you are of such a disposition.

Mrs. Townly:

Listen! Is my disposition really so horrible?

Lucas:

More than I care to suffer.

Mrs. Townly:

At bottom, I'm really no good?

Lucas:

To be fair, I know that it isn't from malice that you torment the whole world—but your will is naturally contrary and never agrees with the will of any other person.

Mrs. Townly:

You hold a strange opinion of me—for of all the women in the world, there isn't one who contradicts less than I do.

Lucas:

There's nobody like you, it's true.

Mrs. Townly:

I never contradict except for good reason. But I don't

like being contradicted. For example, I'm angry with you for your obstinacy. Why do you obstinately hide from me that which I wish to know? Don't I know that you are the advisor, the oracle of my husband? Without a doubt he has taken you into his confidence in the plan he has for Angelica.

Lucas:

Hey! He did speak to me about that.

Mrs. Townly:

Ha! Tell me about it.

Lucas:

I considered the matter of Miss Angelica very thoroughly.

Mrs. Townly:

Yes.

Lucas:

I know what I would tell myself about that matter.

Mrs. Townly:

Well, Lucas?

Lucas:

But my thoughts, your husband's thoughts, your daughter's thoughts—I'm not going to tell you. Not even if you cry.

Mrs. Townly:

Lucas, I beg you, tell me.

Lucas:

You're not going to find out a thing. I see you coming. You're always trying to find out the yes and the no. I will marry her. I will not marry her. What did he say? What did she say? And all that just so you can see the road others are taking so you can cross them.

Mrs. Townly:

On the contrary, I am always going the right way, and each of you turns away from me from malice. And in a word, I know they have made some plan contrary to mine. But I see my daughter coming and I must talk to her again. Halloo, Angelica, halloo. Come here for a minute.

Lucas: (exiting)

I am going to see Mr. Townly in the arbor.

Angelica: (entering)

What do you want me for, mother?

Mrs. Townly:

To speak to you again, daughter.

Angelica:

I'm always ready to listen to you.

Mrs. Townly:

I can complain about you every way because you are a dissimulator, while I am good and reasonable. Since I have to dispose of you one way or another, I want to consult your inclinations. Speak sincerely for once in your life. Do you want to marry or not?

Angelica:

I've already told you mother, I am duty bound not to have any will in this matter.

Mrs. Townly:

But you do, nevertheless—admit it. I have no end other than your satisfaction. Open your heart to me: speak naturally. You think that marriage can make a girl happy?

Angelica:

I see some wives who praise their situation.

Mrs. Townly:

Ah, now I begin to understand.

Angelica:

But I see others who complain.

Mrs. Townly:

I don't understand you. Speak to me a little. You've seen this newlywed who goes from door to door boasting about her good luck. Do you hear her with pleasure?

Angelica:

Yes, indeed, mother.

Mrs. Townly:

You wish, then, to be married?

Angelica:

Not at all. For this same woman the other day afflicted by her complaints the same assembly that she had recently regaled the day before with praises of her husband.

Mrs. Townly:

So you mean you're afraid to take the risk of getting married?

Angelica:

I didn't say that, mother.

Mrs. Townly:

What are you saying? Either you think marriage is good or bad—you long for it or you dread it.

Angelica:

I don't long for it and I don't dread it. I've only voiced some simple reflections without taking one side or the other. The pros and cons seem pretty well balanced to me. That's what has suspended my choice up to now.

Mrs. Townly:

Your indecision begins to make me impatient. You have too much character to remain in a situation so indolent.

Angelica:

That's the situation a young girl ought to remain in until her mother can decide for her without difficulty.

Mrs. Townly:

But if I decided to marry you?

Angelica:

My reasons for marrying would become stronger, for the reason that my duty would make me forget all the contrary arguments.

Mrs. Townly:

And if I decide to keep you single?

Angelica:

Then the reasons against marriage would appear to me to be the best.

Mrs. Townly:

What talk, what a tractable spirit. I cannot get it out of you. What? You won't give me the pleasure of knowing your inclination.

Angelica:

My inclination is to follow yours.

Mrs. Townly:

She won't give up her opinion.

Angelica:

I will obey you to the death.

Mrs. Townly:

What obstinacy, what an opinionated—

Angelica:

It's not obstinacy.

Mrs. Townly:

What, you contradict me without stopping?

Angelica:

To wish what you wish is to contradict you?

Mrs. Townly:

Yes, yes, yes, because I want you to express your will and you won't do it.

Angelica:

But, Mother!

Mrs. Townly:

You make me beside myself. Shut up. They will all say I'm wrong again. Now it's you—yes, it's your spirit, if one can call it that—a spirit of contradiction. I don't know how I can live with you. A daughter like this is a real domestic calamity. I want to get rid of you for sure. Yes, miss—I will marry you off today. The two candidates are Edward Richly on one side, and Mr. Nelson on the other. I will not give you the honor, I will not give you the choice. You will take the one I choose. I will speak to your father one more time. If his ideas are reasonable, I will agree. If not, no.

(Exit Mrs. Townly in a rage)

Angelica: (sighing)

What violence is necessary to turn me into a dissimulator with all the world? I am naturally sincere. But where my mother is concerned, I don't dare confide in anyone if I'm in a situation where I can see what's happening.

(Enter Mr. Edward Richly)

Edward:

Here I am again, young lady, and I've resolved not to return to Oxford without having first had an explanation with you. I swear to you your manners make me beside myself. I am furious; worse, I'm no longer in possession of myself. When I think that since the last time I came here, neither my love, nor my respect, nor my prayers, nor my reproaches, have succeeded in getting one word out of you. (pause) I can't make any sense out of it. When I spoke to you of the most violent passion that ever was, you listened to me with a tranquility, a languor that was incomprehensible. For women react either with love or scorn or anger to such emotions. Just Heavens, what am I to think of a silence so obstinate?

Angelica:

Only that I am prudent and nothing more.

Edward:

Do you approve of my love or forbid it?

Angelica:

I can't say.

Edward:

Always the same indifferent tone.

Angelica:

You haven't been able to tell whether I have any inclination for you, right?

Edward:

That's what upsets me.

Angelica:

Nor have you seen any aversion?

Edward:

No indeed. But that's not satisfactory.

Angelica:

It satisfies me. For I have need to be impenetrable to your curiosity. Didn't I tell you that I have formed a project to secure my freedom, and that to implement this project, it is necessary that my mother be unable to tell whether I love you or someone else? My father must also be kept from the truth—and therefore you also must be kept in the dark—for if you know it, my father, my mother, and anyone who sees you will be well informed.

Edward:

You're trying to tell me I'm indiscreet?

Angelica:

No, but your vivacity takes the place of indiscretion.

Edward:

I know how to control my temperament. For example, from the moment I saw you I felt possessed to such a degree that you wouldn't think it possible. And I swear to you that a word of enlightenment—one little word from you—will make me just as tranquil as you are.

Angelica:

But suppose the word is that I have no intention of marrying you?

Edward:

Ah, so that is what you dare to tell me? How can I listen to such infamy? Just Heaven!

Angelica:

You're not tranquil: would you feel better if I promised never to marry anyone but you?

Edward:

If you promised me that—ah! I'd die of delight. Yes, my joy would be so great—

Angelica:

So that you would publish that, too. See how your transports of joy or despair give away everything! They would divulge my secret, and from them my mother would know what I want to do: then she would cross me furiously.

Thus I find that I am wise to keep you ignorant of my true intentions.

Edward:

I can't be ignorant of them, ingrate. They are so plain. So I tell you, I've just learned you will be betrothed to Mr. Nelson today.

Angelica:

That is possibly true.

Edward:

And that's why I came here.

Angelica:

Well, go away, then.

Edward:

And that is what has made me understand all your politics. I see you've managed me up to this point because I am friends with your mother. You fear that, irritated by your refusal, I will prevent this marriage.

Angelica:

Prevent this marriage! I believe you are a very gallant man to prevent me from securing my advantage.

Edward:

No, cruel woman, no. Don't worry. If you are happy with another, I will die, but I will not prevent you.

Angelica:

You are ruining my plans already. But I do believe that if I had no inclination for you, you wouldn't try to force my feelings. Do what I want you to do. Don't see either my father or my mother today. I forbid you to appear here. So go, I beg you.

Edward:

I obey you blindly, but if you betray me—

Angelica:

I cannot betray you, because I've promised you nothing.

Edward:

If you betray me, you are the most cruel, the most—

Angelica:

Oh, if you are going to berate me, wait till I've done something. And I will do something very soon perhaps. Don't be so impatient.

Edward:

WHAT! You mean—?

Angelica:

Here is my father. Leave quickly.

(Exit Edward)

(Enter Mr. Townly from another direction)

Townly:

Rejoice, little girl, rejoice. You will be married according to my wishes. I have triumphed and put it over on your mother.

Angelica:

Ah, poor papa, I am afraid indeed that—

Townly: (dancing around)

I put it over on her, I tell you. She just insisted herself that I do what I wish. And I had to appear not to like it for fear she'd change her mind.

Angelica:

Once she gets an idea, action soon follows.

Townly:

Yes, my darling daughter, the great wealth of Mr. Nelson is as pleasing to my wife as it is to myself. A rich merchant is a treasure for a girl like you who hasn't a romantic thought in her head. True, he's a bit rustic and crude, but he's open, honest.

Angelica:

I pardon this crudeness in favor of his honesty.

Townly:

Some say he lacks good qualities, but I find he has many. If only he could get away from the habit of saying things which have neither rhyme nor reason. He's a little too familiar, especially with women he's never met before.

(Enter Mr. Nelsonm sporting a large gold vest, huge cuffs, a big belly; his fingers are covered with rings)

Nelson:

Hey, neighbor—well, well, your old lady says that—what didn't she say, that woman? Ha! There's your daughter. Well, well, when shall we get married, honey?

Angelica:

I have no idea.

Townly:

Not everything's ready yet.

Nelson:

Ready, ready, I'm ready. Yes, yes, Angie, I give you my word. Take the biggest ring from my finger—it's yours.

Angelica:

We aren't at the altar yet.

Townly:

We have to consider.

Nelson:

Let's consider, let's consider.

Angelica:

We must take precautions.

Nelson: (grabbing her hand)

Take, take.

Angelica:

While you are deliberating, it's better that I stay with my mother.

Townly:

Go quickly. We haven't any time to lose.

Nelson:

Time is pressing, yes. (squeezing her) Wait, wait, I want to see you again. It makes me feel good. Let's talk about any old thing. Tell me a story.

Angelica:

What sort of story do you want me to tell you?

Nelson:

Well, tell me, tell me—you're cute, sweetie—tell me a little story—

Angelica:

It's time that I should go—

Nelson: (still holding her by the arm)

Ho, I want you to tell me— Ah, I love you with all my heart—tell me a little love story.

Angelica:

You love me, and I'm obliged to you for that. Story's over.

Nelson:

Well, the story's over. Why did you tell me that story? Tell me instead—

Townly: (separating them)

Oh, let her go. It really is important that her mother not see her with us.

Nelson:

Go then. Go darling. Get ready to be my wife.

(Exit Angelica)

Townly:

Let's discuss a little how we are going to manage my wife. For that's the difficulty in our little business.

Nelson:

What's the problem?

Townly:

Not really a problem, but—

Nelson:

Because it's not a problem for me—

Townly:

Do you have some expedient to—?

Nelson:

Sure, sure, leave that to me. Tell me, what are you going to do?

Townly:

That's the problem, I tell you.

Nelson:

You, you, you are a poor planner. Nothing is so easy.

Townly:

Instruct me then!

Nelson:

Nothing is so easy. Now how do you intend to go about it?

Townly:

That's what puzzles me.

Nelson:

But, but, but, me too— She's a terrible woman, your wife.

Townly:

I see we're both too clever and cunning to figure out what to do. But, by luck, I have a gardener who has more clever ideas that anybody in the world. He should be a statesman. A real good head on his shoulders.

Nelson:

I've got a good head, too. Have him here and we'll figure it out.

Townly:

Here he is now.

(Enter Lucas)

Townly:

Well, Lucas, have you been thinking about our business—have you considered what I said to you?

Lucas:

Shh!

Townly:

Shh?

Nelson:

Shh!

Lucas:

This gentleman here wishes to marry Miss Angelica, Angelica also, Madam does, you do, and so do I. So the matter's settled.

Nelson:

See—it's settled.

Lucas:

I say it's not settled. For from the moment she sees that we want it, too—she won't stand for it, not her!

Townly:

That's the trouble.

Nelson:

That's the trouble.

Lucas:

Oh, I ask you if—

Townly:

Certainly.

Nelson:

What a question.

Lucas:

I ask you then if she were unaware that we agree—

Nelson:

That's a good idea.

Townly:

Very good, Lucas.

Nelson:

That's my advice.

Lucas:

That's good advice. You must tell everybody so that your opinion's spread by rumor. For my part, I know that your wife's temper is like a whirligig that's always turning one way, then another in the wind. Therefore, we must make the wind appear to blow from the West so she'll blow to the East. Ah, there must be two winds blowing about Miss Angelica. Nelson on one side, and Young Richly on the other. We have only to say that it's Richly we want, and she will force this gentleman on us just to cross us. That's my pronouncement.

Townly:

That will tie it up.

Nelson:

That's the trick. Here are a hundred pounds, Lucas.

Lucas:

It's necessary to tie two knots to do the job right. For there remains the little matter of putting Madam in the mood to cross you.

Townly:

Let's try to do it immediately—our lawyer has been called, the marriage contract is ready.

Lucas:

Yes, but to finish this properly she must be put into a rage. I know the secret of irritating her. When she comes to inspect my garden, I will pretend not to say a word. Instead, I will scrape the ground with my shovel—that will infuriate her. I will shake my head—she'll take that for opposition and begin to argue; the fire will ignite, and when her spirit is aflame—she will remember that she is an honest woman and that she told you and you deceived her. And here she is now. I will get her going, then you come in and announce you've decided on Young Richly.

(Exit Nelson and Townly, then enter Mrs. Townly)

Mrs. Townly:

You were there quite a while with my husband. Apparently, he knows the one he wants for a son-in-law. Is it Mr. Richly or Mr. Nelson, as I advised him?

Lucas: (turning his hat)

HMMM!

Mrs. Townly:

You turn your hat. That means my husband didn't take my advice.

Lucas: (shaking his head)

PRRR!

Mrs. Townly:

Mr. Nelson, you say is not to my husband's taste—and he prefers Richly?

Lucas:

Heh, heh, heh.

Mrs. Townly:

Because he is younger? Or because Richly is more pleasing to my daughter?

Lucas:

Oh, well—

Mrs. Townly:

What! You think that the solid wealth of Mr. Nelson is not preferable—

Lucas:

Well—

Mrs. Townly:

I get mad when I hear nonsense like this.

Lucas:

But, but, but—

Mrs. Townly:

False reasoning, all of it.

Lucas: (striking the ground with his foot)

The devil!

Mrs. Townly:

And everything you have told me is what my husband told you?

Lucas:

Pah fan goo.

Mrs. Townly:

So you've told me word for word everything he said. Well, let me tell you, in spite of him—

Lucas:

Han.

Mrs. Townly:

Yes, in spite of him. In his teeth.

Lucas:

Pao.

Mrs. Townly:

Yes. He takes a highhanded tone like that with me.

Lucas:

Pa, ta, ta.

Mrs. Townly:

He will see that I am the boss.

Lucas:

Puff.

Mrs. Townly:

Oh, that's too much. Husband, you cross me, you insult me, you outrage me!

(Lucas signals Townly to come in and places Townly beside his wife; Lucas exits)

Mrs. Townly: (seeing him after a moment in Lucas' place)

Continue, sir, continue. I really want to know where you get the things you say to me.

Townly:

I didn't say a word.

Mrs. Townly:

Go ahead, be brave. It takes a lot to get me worked up.

Townly:

It's true that I've come to speak to you.

Mrs. Townly:

To speak to me without reason, without sense, that Mr. Nelson wouldn't be good for my daughter.

Townly:

Still, Richly—

Mrs. Townly:

Don't say another word—

Townly:

I ask you to consider Richly.

Mrs. Townly:

No, sir. Richly presents nothing worthy of my consideration.

Townly:

Well, for my sake then—

Mrs. Townly:

From today, I give my daughter to Mr. Nelson.

Townly:

But the reason?

Mrs. Townly:

The reason is that I wish it. And to prove that I am right, it's going to happen as I wish and immediately. Mr. Nelson is here. Get ready to sign the papers.

(Exit Mrs. Townly to the house, and after a moment enter Lucas)

Townly:

Well—did I play my part well?

Lucas:

Like an expert this time. She is going to do what we want willingly and for the first time in her life.

Townly:

There—is the lawyer here?

Lucas:

I'll go see. And when I see her, I am going to tell her I like Richly better. To add a little fuel to the fire.

(Exit Lucas)

(Enter Angelica)

Townly:

We've done wonderfully, daughter.

Angelica:

I've heard. I was under the swing with the lawyer—he's just come. It's time and he's on schedule.

Townly:

I am going to speak to him. Go quickly and rejoin your mother.

(Exit Townly)

Angelica:

Things are at the point where I wish them. And the measures I have taken will succeed. Watch and see what happens.

(Exit Angelica; after a moment enter Mrs. Townly and a Lackey)

Mrs. Townly:

Tell me child, where did you get this letter from? Who is your master?

Lackey:

I am forbidden to tell you that—and to prevent you from forcing it out of me, I am leaving right away.

(Exit Lackey)

Mrs. Townly:

Now what's this mystery?

(Reading low)

Hmm, hmm, hmm. "I advise you that your daughter is in communication with Mr. Nelson and wants to marry him and to make you sign the wedding contract, they have a lawyer ready who will appear as if by chance." Indeed, that's the lawyer I just saw with Angelica. The warning is obviously true. "In a word, your husband pretended not to want Nelson so you would prefer him." So! Mr. Nelson is the choice of my husband.

(Enter Lucas and Townly)

Lucas:

Courage, sir. Tell her quickly that I am against Mr. Nelson.

Townly:

Listen, my dear wife—

Lucas:

I tell you that—

Townly:

I want you to know that—

Lucas: (to Mrs. Townly)

That I and your husband—

Townly:

You say that you want Mr. Nelson for a son-in-law, right? I tell you that my daughter doesn't want him.

Lucas:

The matter is a little delicate.

Mrs. Townly:

It isn't my daughter's will or mine that ought to decide—it's yours, my husband—and in this and in everything else, you are master.

Lucas:

As for me, I think—

Mrs. Townly:

You're a good advisor, Lucas, and I willingly listen to your advice.

Townly:

In a word, my wife, you have proposed Mr. Nelson to me, and I don't want him.

Mrs. Townly:

Let's speak softly. I love peace and harmony. I will do whatever you find most agreeable.

Townly: (aloud)

What's agreeable to me is—

(low)

—not to have such complaisance about this.

Mrs. Townly:

To me it's to have a husband that I love and respect.

Townly:

You're joking, but I tell you Mr. Nelson is not to my taste.

Mrs. Townly:

Your taste determines mine, and I tell you I won't give another thought to Mr. Nelson.

Townly:

Lucas?

Lucas: (low)

Try harder. Her contradictory spirit isn't on fire yet.

Townly:

Tell me, Madam, are you making fun of me?

Mrs. Townly:

But what makes you think that when I give you my word?

Lucas:

Good! Your word comes and goes like the air.

Mrs. Townly: (sweetly)

Wait till you see.

Lucas:

You can't make up your mind.

Mrs. Townly:

To prove my sincerity and my submission, I am going this moment to forbid Mr. Nelson to set foot in this house.

(Exit Mrs. Townly)

Townly:

I believe she's going to do it. What should have caused this miracle?

Lucas:

Listen, it must be that—

Townly:

It would be just my luck. The only time in her life she doesn't contradict me, it's to contradict me.

Lucas:

For her to obey you is not natural.

Townly:

I am going to see what's happening. I still don't believe it.

(Exit Townly)

Nelson: (entering)

Well, well, Lucas. We are going to sign the contract. Here's the money I promised you—

Lucas:

Madam is going to give you your walking papers— she's looking for you to do just that.

Nelson:

She doesn't want me, you say?

Lucas:

Something has happened, I don't know exactly what. Wait for me here, I'm going to see for myself.

(Exit Lucas)

Nelson:

I love waiting for this little Angelica—but I'm joking about that. If I don't marry her, I can marry at least four others.

(Enter Angelica followed by Edward, who is determined to fathom her tricks)

Nelson:

Well, well, poor girl, it's bad for you. You won't get married.

Angelica:

What an irritating thing.

Nelson:

It makes me mad, but I'm easy. You're crying because you love me, and that's swell. Don't cry, come on, don't cry. You'll make me do it, too.

Angelica:

Go quickly, join my father, second him, speak together to my mother. Beg her. Press her.

Nelson:

Shh! Shh! There's your other lover, who's listening.

Angelica:

Ha—are you there, Mr. Richly?

Edward:

What I've just heard, what you've just said, has exposed you to me. The lawyer I've just been with proved sufficiently your betrayal, but you aren't worthy of my reproaches. I will take the way of scorn and silence.

(Shouting)

Don't wait for me, nor beg, nor reproach—ingrate! No, faithless one, no, traitress—

Nelson:

Do you call this the way of silence?

Edward:

Just Heaven—

Nelson:

What are you complaining of? That she promised you something?

Edward:

Nothing at all, Mr. Nelson. I would like to know indeed, sir, by what right you insult me? How, I beg you, can you have any hope? First of all, my father has as much money as you—and the little merit that you have—

Nelson: (showing his hand)

Why, do you see this hand? These five fingers alone are worth more than all your father's wealth.

Angelica:

For me, I prefer Mr. Nelson's good nature to this wild passion which you never give up—

Nelson:

Fie! He's crazy in love—like in a novel.

Angelica:

His kind words touch me more than your despairing face.

Nelson:

I've heard it said that women don't care for the affected, but I pity him. Go, young man, go—console yourself. I will lend you some money.

Edward:

Why, damn you, sir—

Angelica: (taking Edward by the arm)

You're beside yourself. Go away, I beg you. I don't like to be bothered like that.

Nelson:

Hey, me either. I'm going to rejoin your father.

(Low to Angelica)

I order you to get rid of him. Give him his walking papers and come find me.

(Exit Nelson)

Edward:

Your procedure seems to me so outré that I cannot believe that you are feigning. I don't flatter myself, but if you were pretending because Nelson was around—now he is gone—justify yourself!

(Enter Mrs. Townly)

Mrs. Townly: (aside)

My daughter alone with Richly!

Edward:

Justify yourself—or admit you have betrayed me. Speak, we are alone.

Angelica:

I will speak to you just as I spoke in the presence of Mr. Nelson. My father wants me to marry him, and I tell you I am delighted.

Edward:

Oh! I give up. No more explanations. I am going to find your mother.

Angelica:

Go, sir, go, you can tell her that I want no part of you.

Edward: (seeing Mrs. Townly)

Have you heard, Madam? I am betrayed, Madam. For it is no longer time to hide from you my love for this ingrate—you see she has betrayed me.

Mrs. Townly:

I feel sorry for you, sir. You see father and daughter plotted against you, and me, too. I enter into your feelings because I always sympathize with the feelings of others.

Edward:

No. After what she's done, I never wish to speak of her again.

Mrs. Townly:

I swear to you I have no objection to your proposing to my daughter.

Edward:

You propose her to me in vain.

Mrs. Townly:

But to prove to you, a reasonable man, that reason alone guides me in all I do—I wish to offer you—

Edward:

I refuse your offers, Madam. I am not a man to force her inclinations.

Mrs. Townly:

So that I may have the pleasure of avenging you on my husband, on my daughter—on all those who conspire to contradict me—I beg you, sir.

Edward:

Can't do it.

Mrs. Townly:

What! You contradict me, too? Oh, I will do so much for you, if you will marry my daughter!

Angelica:

What! Mother! You wouldn't marry me against my will?

Mrs. Townly:

Against your will, daughter? Don't think of it—because you have no will, remember?

Angelica:

Alas, when I spoke to you thus, I didn't speak sincerely. Why will you prevent a rich match with Mr. Nelson?

Mrs. Townly:

He's got more wealth than you deserve.

Angelica:

Hey, mother, I beg you—

Mrs. Townly:

Shut up! I know all your tricks. The lawyer told me everything. You wanted to betray me. To expose me to the will of a husband! To punish you, I will make you sign the contract you drew up against me. Only, I'm going to fill in the name of Richly.

(Exit Mrs. Townly)

Edward:

No, Madam, I will never sign. I prefer to die rather than marry your daughter.

Angelica: (imitating him)

"I prefer to die rather than marry your daughter—" You say it very naturally.

Edward:

As I feel it, ingrate.

Angelica:

And as I wished it. For if you had done it to persuade my mother, it wouldn't have worked, for it wouldn't have sounded right. You could not have deceived her if you hadn't been deceived yourself.

Edward:

Explain yourself.

Angelica:

To make my mother agree to what I want, it was also necessary to deceive my father. He tried to trick her naturally enough, and when I saw how they were working for Mr. Nelson, by pretending the contrary, I sent her an anonymous letter explaining what they were up to. And it did the trick. Seeing all the world against you, she has taken your part—and wishes to make us marry to contradict them—and you, too.

Edward:

Can what I hear be true? Misfortune overwhelms me, and joy confounds me. But I don't know which.

Angelica:

I don't want you to show it until after the signature. I fear some indiscreet transport of joy. No, Edward, don't believe yet that I love you.

Edward: (wildly)

Ah! Darling Angelica—divine lady—

Angelica:

Someone's coming. Keep pretending.

(Enter Lucas)

Angelica:

No, Edward, no. I will not be married to you against my will.

Lucas:

No, dammit, it will not be against your will—for you'll marry him with joy. But it may not happen yet, for I doubt you can both scheme together or that you can pretend to be pretending. Your mother's on her way, but I've warned you so that you may deceive her.

Angelica:

Ah! Heavens.

Edward:

How wretched you are!

Lucas:

For you it will be wretched. For Madam changes her mind quickly if she suspects for a minute that you want it too. That's too bad, 'cause Mr. Nelson promised me a hundred pounds.

Edward:

You rogue. Why didn't you ask for two hundred from me?

Lucas:

There's no time. Madam knows all. Meanwhile, if I take your money, it will be true that Madam knows all—for dammit, she knows nothing.

Angelica:

Ah, my poor Lucas.

Edward:

Wait, take my purse.

Lucas:

And here comes Madam returning. I am going to assist you.

(Enter Mrs. Townly, Mr. Townly, Mr. Nelson, and the lawyer)

Lucas:

Come quickly, Madam, see the young folks are fighting. Come quickly, separate them. They find everything the other one says enraging—so much so that I would think they are already married.

Mrs. Townly:

Does my daughter revolt against me! Insolent! You here, too, sir.

(To Nelson)

Leave instantly.

Nelson:

Go, go. I am more complacent than you. You kick me out and I'm leaving.

Mrs. Townly:

You're a brute.

Nelson:

Goodbye, old battle cruiser.

Mrs. Townly:

A booby, a simpleton.

Nelson:

I never contradict anyone.

(Exit Nelson)

Townly:

Really, my dear wife—

Mrs. Townly:

Shut up, my dear husband—

Lawyer:

May I dare explain to you, Madam—

Mrs. Townly:

I am delighted that you are all against young Richly.

He lacked only you. Give me the contract that I may sign—

(signing) Come, Angelica, sign after me. Obey me.

Angelica: (signing)

I still can't be married, because my father won't sign, so there.

Mrs. Townly: (to Edward)

To oblige you, sir, I have put a gift for you in the contract.

Edward: (signing)

Hey! I didn't do it because of the gift. Go ahead, sir, don't waste a minute for fear Madam will change her mind.

(Townly pushed by his wife, signs)

Lawyer:

These proceedings are closed. (Folds up the contract, bows and exits)

(Lucas whispers to Mrs. Townly)

Mrs. Townly:

What do you say?

Lucas:

I wish to say simply that they love each other.

Townly:

And I only wanted to marry her. No matter to whom.

Mrs. Townly:

I've been betrayed.

Angelica:

I throw myself at your feet, Mama.

Edward:

A thousand pardons, Madam.

Mrs. Townly:

I will never pardon you in my life.

Townly:

You signed.

Mrs. Townly:

Yes, but I will disinherit her. I will never see my son-in-law again. I will divorce my husband. I will hang Lucas and the lawyer. I am going crazy.

(Mrs. Townly runs out in a fury)

Edward:

We'd better bring her back before she does something dangerous.

Townly:

So much for the spirit of contradiction.

CURTAIN

THE DOUBLE WIDOWING

CAST OF CHARACTERS

The Countess, an imperious woman of no particular age

Mr. Bramble, her steward

Widow, Bramble's wife

Tuneless, the Countess's butler who composes music

Desmond, Mr. Bramble's nephew, a sentimentalist in love with Arabella

Arabella, the Widow's niece, a rationalist in love with Desmond

Maid, the Countess's maid

Lucy, the Widow's maid

Mr. MacPherson, a servant of the Countess

Mrs. MacPherson, his wife

Four men, six women

ACT I

A room in the Countess's country house. The time is the early eighteenth century.

Lucy

I am delighted to see you return, sir. I've been looking for you all over the place, in the gardens, everywhere.

Desmond

Good day, Lucy, good day.

Lucy

You've come at just the right time. The Countess and I and all the house have been waiting for you to return with great impatience. But, quickly, tell me news of your uncle— Is Mr. Bramble dead or alive?

Desmond

I know nothing of it.

Lucy

We are in the same incertitude. Only Mrs. Bramble is certain. We've told her he's dead for sure, to make her fall into the trap we've set for her. She thinks she's a widow, and it's on that belief that we build our little project of your marriage, sir.

Desmond

What's that?

Lucy

I told you, that to facilitate your marriage with Arabella, the Countess, who protects you both, has pulled a thousand strings to prove to my mistress that your uncle is dead. Mrs. Bramble is so sure of being a widow that she put on mourning yesterday, sir.

Desmond

What are you telling me?

Lucy

I'm telling you business that concerns both of us. For the thirty gold crowns you promised me has the same appeal to me that Arabella has for you. Listen to me, then. To help us, you must hide from our widow the love you have for Arabella, for if she suspects you love her niece—

Desmond

I know all that. I've been through it just now with the Countess.

Lucy

Sir, pardon my useless talk. I ought first to talk of the charms of this young beauty who—

Desmond

What charms she has, Lucy, what charms! She has so many!

Lucy

The most pretty little charms. Not fifteen years old, these charms, and new ones added every day. And, you will marry all of them soon.

Desmond

It's the greatest misfortune that can happen to me.

Lucy

A misfortune to possess something you love so much! Here's one of your bizarre refinements. You are the most reasonable gentleman in England, but you've no common sense. Speak to me reasonably: do you wish to marry her?

Desmond

Do I ever wish it!

Lucy

If you wish this marriage ardently, let's work in concert. I hope Arabella will be your wife today.

Desmond

Alas, that's what I fear.

Lucy

Again! Oh, you exaggerate. Is this crazy love or simply craziness?

Desmond

No, Lucy, no, it is not caprice, it is not exaggeration. I fear with my mind that which I want with all my heart. I am well aware that I cannot live without the adorable Arabella. But, I foresee we will be unhappy together. In a word, we are unable to agree about anything.

Lucy

And, what is it necessary to agree about to get married?

Desmond

If you knew the reception she just gave me—

Lucy

She was wrong—

Desmond

She received me with an air—

Lucy

Is it possible?

Desmond

After eight days' absence.

Lucy

She received you coldly?

Desmond

She received me shouting, dancing. I saw her jump about with happiness.

Lucy

My word, you're not wise. What! You despair because she's delighted to see you?

Desmond

Delighted to see me! I cannot compare that dissipated delight with the sensitive pleasure and passion the sight of a loved one should inspire. For example, from the moment I saw her I stood immobile, seized by a languor, my heart beat, my eyes clouded. Ahh! That's the way to express passion. But she is incapable of such a solid, passionate love, which is the only kind that can content me.

Lucy

If I was a man, I'd choose for my wife a woman who was always gay, never moody or sensitive.

Desmond

I want sensibility.

Lucy

In a mistress—but in a wife, shame!

Desmond

It's all an amusement.

Lucy

It's an amusement very dangerous for the husband.

Desmond

One can have feelings and be virtuous.

Lucy

Virtue doesn't always make a woman faithful. I'd like a woman better who had no passions, rather than one who is governed by them.

(Enter Arabella, singing.)

Arabella

La, la, la, la—la, la, la, la, la.

Desmond

Do you hear, Lucy, do you hear?

Lucy

She has a nice voice, doesn't she?

Desmond

After having seen me before being overcome by emotion—

Arabella

La, la, la, la, la, la, la, la.

Desmond (walking away)

I am outraged to hear that.

Arabella

Hey! Here you both are. You don't see what's going on here because you're wrapped up in your somber mood.

Desmond

My emotion is well-justified.

Arabella

You are angry to see me laugh, and I am laughing to see you angry.

Desmond

Is this a way to talk of love?

Arabella

As for love, will yours always be so afflicted?

Desmond

If I had less refinement—

Arabella

You would be more reasonable.

Desmond

Is there anything more reasonable than my complaints?

Arabella

Oh, your exaggerations are always full of reason. But they don't make you happy.

Desmond

What a conversation. Alas, how different your character is from mine.

Arabella

Marriage will solve all that.

Desmond

There, Lucy, I ask you to judge—

Lucy

I have nothing to gain by judging. Judge yourselves. I am going to get my mistress up.

Arabella

Dress her quickly, for the Countess wants to see her right away.

Lucy

Your aunt Bramble is not yet awake, and between the wake up and the coming down of a middle-aged woman, there are numerous ceremonies of the toilette.

(Exit Lucy.)

Arabella

We've got to get some money from my aunt. It's essential.

Desmond

The essential thing is to find out if we're going to be happy together.

Arabella

Nice question! With this type of humor we're going to get along fine; and I'm going to get rid of all your peculiarities.

Desmond

I am not being peculiar, when, after quiet reasoning, I conclude that your frivolousness—

Arabella

Oh, my frivolousness, my frivolousness; I believe that

my gaiety ought to prove my tenderness. Here's how I think you ought to have reasoned, knowing me, and my fear of marriage because it is sad. I naturally fear marriage. I see they want to marry me to you, and I show no emotion. Well, to be gay under these circumstances, doesn't that prove I love you?

Desmond

That's not to hate me.

Arabella

If you don't want me to hate you, don't anger me anymore with the tone you're taking. Seems to me, I love you passably well.

Desmond

Passably. That's a very touching expression, "Passably."

Arabella

Oh I wish you could count the joys I feel.

Desmond

That joy would be properly expressed if you were sure our marriage will succeed, but in the situation we are in, you ought to tremble. And if you were in love, you'd be like me: ill at ease, agitated, in a cruel uncertainty, languishing, sighing, trembling.

(Enter the Countess and her Maid.)

Countess

Well, Arabella, I am working to marry you—aren't you delighted?

Arabella

On the contrary, Madame, I am ill at ease, agitated, and in a cruel uncertainty, languishing, sighing, and trembling. Is that how I should love, sir?

Countess

Enough, Arabella, enough. Desmond, it was I who told her to tease you a bit over your emotionalism. It's not that I don't esteem you highly; the interest I take in your marriage proves that. But today, I've resolved to laugh, and to ridicule all those who happen to be around me. I have nothing but a boring day to pass in the country, and I am gong to amuse myself at the expense of anyone who happens to be around. So beware. Our widow will be the principal subject of my diversion, and the way I intend to get the money out of Mrs. Bramble is a comedy which will amuse me immensely.

Arabella

If you are able to get money out of aunt Bramble, don't mock her. We must pity the afflicted.

Countess

When her husband's death was announced to her, I perceived that only her facial expression showed any signs of affliction.

Desmond

Maybe so, but I beg you to spare her. For if her affection was false, that of my uncle was true enough. And my uncle had the honor to be your steward.

Countess

Oh, Bramble's enriched himself at my expense, and now I will laugh at the expense of his widow. After all, it's an outrage. She wants to disinherit her niece who's my godchild; in a word, she hates what you love. Why manipulate, if it weren't for love of you?

Desmond

If she's done it from love of me, it's an inexcusable folly.

Countess

A less excusable folly is the speed with which she took to mourning yesterday. (to Maid) Miss, tell me how she has been able to find so much crepe in the country?

Maid

I heard this morning from Lucy, that she's always kept a mourning outfit hidden in her trunk, so as always to be well prepared for the unexpected death of her husband. She says every well-ordered wife ought to do the same, so she can celebrate her misfortune from the very first moment of widowhood.

Countess

And you don't want me to ridicule such an affectation? There, Desmond! Go, put on mourning, too, to prove that your uncle is dead.

Arabella

I am also going to put on black, to make it all more touching.

(Exit Arabella and Desmond.)

Countess

Miss, you will have to sing a little aria in the opera that Mr. Tuneless is preparing for me. It's right that my servants contribute to my amusements today.

Maid

I wish your Scotsman were here. He sings well. His wife is also a good singer, and dances well for a Highlander.

Countess

Here she is now. What does she wish to tell me?

(Enter Mrs. MacPherson.)

Mrs. MacPherson

Rejoice, Madame, my husband has just returned from Tunbridge Wells.

Countess

I am delighted. He will tell us if Mr. Bramble is dead or alive. He hasn't already told you, has he?

Mrs. MacPherson

My husband never tells me his secrets. He's right, for I am too much of a gossip. I like it better when he tells me nothing, because he's so pompous when he tells me a secret. He has such long oaths, so long that I would as soon listen to a hundred sighs from another man, before he will tell me one word!

Countess

Why doesn't he come then?

Mrs. MacPherson

Madame, to appear to you in his proper attire, he has

gone to have his wig curled and powdered.

Maid

He's rouging also. For he went to the Wells to lighten his skin.

Mrs. MacPherson

Don't mock him before her, ma'am. He went to the waters to improve his health. And to please me, for he loves me, and I am determined that he be healthy.

Countess

I am delighted to see you in such good humor.

Mrs. MacPherson

I am happy because my husband has returned. And also, because your servant has been slipping us a little wine, discreetly. Women from my country are born for wine, like the French are born for love. Each to his custom, and often enough the one does not impede the other.

Maid

Here is Mr. MacPherson, Madame. You are going to hear an interesting speech, because he's erudite, your Highlander.

MacPherson (entering)

Madame, Madame.

Countess

Don't waste your time bowing. Tell me—is Bramble dead?

MacPherson

I know all about these matters, in extreme exactitude.

Countess

All these things consist in one word: he's dead, or he isn't.

MacPherson

It is necessary to explain all these things to you by direction. For, when I left you, you directed that I should bring you a report of all the circumstances of our trip in writing.

Countess

Very well. What I want to know is written in your journal.

MacPherson

My journal consists of words without paper. For I have written in my mind in three little chapters our departure, our trip, our return.

Countess

Here's a well-ordered explanation.

MacPherson

With regard to the first, Mr. Bramble was very ridiculous, very ridiculous. He said he'd been married to his wife for ten years without children, and it was to cure sterility that he was going to the waters. So much for what he said as soon as he arrived.

Countess

If this story wasn't so funny, it would make me very impatient.

MacPherson

In the second chapter, your bailiff was also very ridiculous. For I like wine, and he went to the waters to drink water, and in this water, he found, in place of virility, illness—so much illness, that he is dying.

Countess

Now, we're at the point. Bramble thought he was dying and is not dead. Listen, you must tell his wife that when her husband was dying, he died.

MacPherson

Ha, ha, ha. When one finds the widow of a living man, we'll have a good laugh.

Countess

When is he coming? Where did you leave him?

MacPherson

I left him yesterday, about thirty leagues from here, when his coach broke down. Go on ahead, he said, for I'm likely to be sick here until tomorrow, and my coach won't be ready till Monday. I will come on Tuesday.

(Exit MacPherson and Mrs. MacPherson.)

Countess

According to that, he won't be here until tomorrow and cannot disturb our project today. So, Miss, tell my dancing women to prepare for the wedding I intend to celebrate today.

Maid

We will do all our best to please you, and though I sing poorly, I can sing a sad song about being a widow.

Countess

It's Tuneless who is getting everything ready. He wants to be a music master, my Butler.

Maid

He's an original. Look here. I believe he's composing, for he's walking to the beat. Hold, hold, Madame, the spirit torments him—he's possessed by the demon of music.

Countess

Shh! He doesn't see us. Let's give him the pleasure—

Tuneless (entering)

Nothing's going right, dammit. La, la, la, la. I can never find a completely new idea. (slowly) La, la, la, la, la—no, that opening's in Lully. La, la, la, la, la, la Lully again. La, la, la, la Lully again. That Lully is everywhere, everywhere I turn. I am very unfortunate not to have been born before him. Everything I have in my head is useless because they say I plagiarize him. La, la, la, la, la good there. La, la, la, la, la. Admirable. La, la. Marvelous. And the second, lower—la, la, la, low tone, what invention. La, la, la, la, la, la, la, la what reflections of genius. The notes are coming to me—write them down quickly. (with one knee on the ground, he writes on some paper on the other knee, until, perceiving the Countess, he takes off his hat in this position and continues to write) (singing)

Pardon me, Madame, oh pardon, Madame, da, de, da, de da, Madame. I note the last tone. (rising and bowing to the Countess) It's a duo for an aria about widowhood, as you have commanded. (giving her a paper.) Wait, Madame, you know how to sing without a book.

Countess

I see Mrs. Bramble in the gallery. I must speak with our widow.

Tuneless

Let us sing together, and that will serve as a rehearsal.

(Exit Countess.)

Tuneless (to Maid)

Now you will represent the widow. Carefully imitate the affliction of widows. Cry with your eyes down in your chin.

Lucy (entering)

Retire. My mistress approaches. She's coming here to cry on the way. She needs practice.

Tuneless

Exactly. Soon she'll be crying for her money. Real tears then.

Lucy

Don't joke. I'm afraid all this may be dangerous for her.

Tuneless

Why is that?

Lucy

I'm sorry for her. When the Countess guaranteed she was a widow, it was like a knife thrust in her heart.

Tuneless

What? She felt the blow?

Lucy

Think what she's going to feel when they undeceive her. The loss of her delightful status of widowhood will cause her to die.

Tuneless

Let's come to the business. Tell me truly, now that she believes her husband is dead—is she in love with Desmond, and does she plan to marry him?

Lucy

She thought about it even while she was alive. And I always thought she prayed the nephew would outlive his uncle.

Tuneless

From the confidences her husband has made to me, I have often thought he destined his niece for the post of her aunt. He was quite explicit that Arabella was the niece of his wife only in the third degree.

Lucy

My mistress wishes that Desmond was not her husband's nephew.

Tuneless

These sentiments astonish me in a woman so careful of the proprieties.

Lucy

She's proper in public, but with certain women, public morals and private morals differ as much as their faces do from the time they get up and the time they go to bed.

Tuneless

Everything considered, I judge that these two are perfectly matched in all the arts of conjugal hypocrisy.

Lucy

They love each other, in proportion to the wealth they hope to obtain from each other.

Tuneless

Yes, self-interest by itself produces more false love in some families than true love produces in all the sincere lovers in London.

Lucy

I admire the wisdom of our law which permits spouses to disinherit one another. For only the hope of inheriting is the dike that can prevent a torrent of family quarrels. Go quickly. Here is my mistress. To gain her confidence, I am going to help her out of her sorrows.

(Exit Tuneless and the Maid. Enter from another direction, the Countess and the Widow Bramble.)

Countess

Save your tears, Madame, save your tears. To tremble, to sigh, to sob. All these demonstrations of sorrow are worse than sorrow itself.

Widow

Alas.

Countess

Don't avoid the offer I'm making you anymore. Respond to me exactly. You don't like to have your niece around. I'm going to take her off your hands and marry her off in the country. Won't you give her some wedding present?

Widow

This is the fourth day of my widowhood—the fourth day isn't it, Lucy?

Lucy

The fourth, yes.

Widow (to Countess)

Well, Madame, since then I haven't had any nourishment at all.

Lucy

We are nourished only by affliction and black tea.

Widow

Everything I eat rests on my stomach like lead.

Lucy

We eat hardly anything, and what we eat suffocates us.

Countess

Answer me, then, Madame, agree.

Widow

No, I won't be alive in four days.

Countess

Live, and don't cry.

Widow

Ah, I will cry more than thirty years.

Lucy

To die soon and cry forever is our final resolution.

Widow

I don't know what I'm saying, Lucy.

Lucy

I see it plainly. We haven't the strength to marry Arabella.

Countess

While your husband was living, you gave the excuse that you hoped to have children. Now, your hopes and excuses are dead with your husband: you are mistress of your estate. You must marry Arabella, or tell me that you don't wish it.

Widow

I cannot make up my mind to marry Arabella. Really, I don't wish her so much ill as to expose her to marriage.

Countess

To hear you speak thus about marriage, one would think you didn't like it.

Widow

On the contrary, it was because my happiness was so perfect, that I don't wish to marry my niece.

Countess

That's a reason to marry her.

Widow

I had a very lovable husband, and I don't want her to have one.

Countess

Explain yourself!

Widow

She will be too overcome if she loses him; to marry her would be to expose her to the risk of becoming a widow.

(cries) And, to unhappiness like mine. Ah, Madame, in the abyss in which I find myself, retreat and solitude, that's the road my niece ought to take.

Countess

Solitude doesn't agree with Arabella.

Widow

Don't speak to me anymore about it. I am too afflicted.

Countess

And, in a word—your niece?

Widow

No, no. I am too afflicted. I intend that she spend her life in a convent.

Countess

From the bad reasons you give me, I discern the good ones you keep to yourself. You wish to protect your money, so you can remarry.

Widow

Me! Me, remarry!

Countess

Listen, to undertake a second marriage, you need the great wealth your husband left you. And, this great wealth, having been earned in managing my affairs—I could—I haven't yet signed off on your husband's accounts—. That's why I beg you not to refuse the ten thousand crowns that you have in your strongbox. I beg you, I really do.

(Exit Countess.)

Widow (ill tempered)

I beg you, she says, I beg you.

Lucy

She begs you with a certain air—

Widow

Taking on a tone—

Lucy

Of people of quality who—

Widow

Believing that their prayers—

Lucy

Are a sort of command. A great lord who asks a citizen to do him a service is like a banker respectfully asking payment on a promissory note.

Widow

She speaks as if one was in great fear of her.

Lucy

You'd have less reason to fear if your husband were

alive. For he was as clever in protecting his prey as he was in catching it.

Widow

Alas, I am indeed lost.

Lucy

Madame, the Countess could easily cheat you. You may say that she cannot cheat the widow of an honest steward, who enriched himself as everyone does by entangling his affairs with hers. But, now she is going to take from you unjustly that which your husband earned on the fair and square.

Widow

That's what I'm afraid of, Lucy.

Lucy

They ought not to oppress widows because they have lost their main support.

Widow

Their support. That's very true, I am without support.

Lucy

Without support! That's why you ought to pacify the

Countess. That way you would peaceably obtain your husband's wealth. Then, find some young man to be your support.

Widow

Ah, Lucy. If I think of accommodating the Countess, it is not to gain peace. But, before I give her anything, I wish to consult with some smart man.

Lucy (low)

Like Desmond. (Aloud) Some smart fellow who—

Widow

Some man of good counsel.

Lucy

Very good.

Widow

A man with a head.

Lucy

By the way, Desmond came this afternoon.

Widow

Desmond's come—?

Lucy

Yes, Madame. He's a smart fellow, Desmond.

Widow

Assuredly.

Lucy

A man of good counsel.

Widow

Without a doubt.

Lucy

A man with a head. If you told him your difficulties—

Widow

He knows my husband's business—

Lucy

Yours will be in good hands.

Widow

Go, tell him that he can find me in the garden.

Lucy

Right away, Madame.

Widow

A wise person ought to take advice.

Lucy

You will follow Desmond's. What wisdom. What wisdom.

CURTAIN

ACT II

Widow

Ah, Lucy, how ashamed I am to tell you of the distant vows I have made to Desmond.

Lucy

So long as those distant vows don't come too soon, I approve of them.

Widow

If I were less virtuous than those ancient wives who could envisage no other consolation except to swallow the ashes of their husbands!

Lucy

You see in your nephew the living features of your husband, his uncle. Catching the possessor of those features will cure you of your scruples.

Widow

Lucy, do you suppose Desmond misunderstands my motives?

Lucy

Not at all. I'm sure he understands them perfectly. But, be discreet. A man understands a widow's hint.

Widow

I have always spoken to him with an indifference, a frigidity—

Lucy

See the fate of virtue—

Widow

I have expressed all the ideas of tenderness with perfect circumspection, but, shrewdly, delicately, with refinement. Really, without these precautions, I would expose myself to continual remorse. I would imagine, without end, that the soul of the departed reproached me. Yes, even in this moment, I hear his complaints, the sound of his voice, actually in my ears.

(Enter Desmond, after Lucy has signaled him to do so.)

Desmond

Madame.

Widow

Ah, Heaven, shh! It's you, Desmond. You've frightened me. I thought I heard the voice of my husband.

Desmond

Really, there's quite a resemblance in our voices. The whole world used to mistake us.

Widow

My husband had a very agreeable voice.

Desmond

Let's talk business.

Widow

The resemblances in families is remarkable. You've got your uncle's manners, even his brusqueness.

Desmond

Following the advice I have given you—

Widow

You have his gestures, his manner, his way of looking. I love most your way of looking—

Desmond

Let's think about finishing.

Widow

What still charms me in my husband is your softness, your wit, your entire person.

Desmond

Madame, I've spoken to the Countess, and I think it's important that you pacify her, but you are not honoring me with your attention.

Widow

With my attention! It's you who don't listen to me.

Desmond

But really, it's wise to give in to her—

Widow

You urge me to give away all my wealth?

Desmond

Only a small part of it. Otherwise, you jeopardize—

Widow

You don't know how much better it would be if I keep it. It would be better for you.

Desmond

For me?

Widow

For, in the future, you understand, sir. I could really, for you— Right, Lucy? I can't explain anymore, sir. You understand, don't you—?

Desmond

I—

Widow

Because propriety prevents me from saying to you—

Lucy

You've told him that already.

Widow

I will say only, that having reflected on what the Countess didn't say, I fear that the husband she intends for Arabella is none other than yourself.

Desmond

Me, Madame?

Lucy

The gentleman would be wiser to go to the source of the wealth.

Widow

I believe it, but from the fear that the Countess will give you, in spite of yourself, to Arabella, I have resolved not to give my money until the marriage contract is signed, and a husband other than yourself is the lucky man. And, I have a thousand other good reasons to communicate to you about this. But, I can't say a word now. Follow me, Lucy.

(Exit Widow.)

Desmond

Lucy.

Lucy

Sir, I have to go.

(Exit Lucy.)

Desmond

What to do now?

(Enter Arabella.)

Arabella

Tell me quickly—how did your conversation go with my aunt?

Desmond

I think I've convinced her that she should let me arbitrate between her and the Countess.

Arabella

That's funny.

Desmond

She's disposed to agree to whatever I suggest, and—in a word—she's working for our marriage, without even knowing it.

Arabella

Without knowing it. That makes me delighted.

Desmond

Do you understand what our happiness is?

Arabella

You will judge against her interest. Nothing could be funnier. It charms me totally.

Desmond

You are pleased by the joke. The humor of it is what touches you. Your first sensation ought to be a passionate feeling of happiness.

Arabella

Happiness touches me, too.

Desmond

Too, too. You have a delightful choice of words—very revealing.

Arabella

Oh, don't quibble with me. I am going to have a good laugh with the Countess.

Desmond

What! Leave me without witnessing—

Arabella

I will witness you wonderfully.

(Enter Lucy.)

Arabella

Ah, Lucy, everything is going wonderfully. You see me in joy. But, in recompense, Desmond is angry. I believe he almost wishes that our marriage should be prevented, and that he will run into some obstacle.

Lucy

Then he can rejoice, for the obstacle has come. Your uncle is returned, sir.

Desmond

My uncle, ah Heaven, I am in despair.

Arabella

All our schemes are ruined. Ah, Desmond, why do you love me so much? It always makes you so unhappy. Really, I feel worse than you—no hope—I am desolated.

Desmond

Desolated, you say?

Arabella

Desolated, desperate.

Desmond

What? You suffer?

Arabella

Oh, how unhappy I am.

Desmond

Ah, what a joy for me! You have feelings. I am loved. I don't want anything else in the world. I want only your heart.

Lucy

You won't have that either.

Desmond

But Lucy, is it really true that my uncle is back? What, in the very moment I was convinced we'd be happy forever. Ah Heaven, is there a misery equal to mine?

(Enter Tuneless.)

Tuneless

The steward is back. What a reversal. He took an express coach and returns just in time to desolate us. His wife's rage is going to rebound on us—for she already knows.

Lucy

For me, I wish them both what they deserve. To the wife, a dead husband. To the husband, a dead wife. At least their desires will not be accomplished quickly.— You will never be married.

Desmond

Here's my uncle coming now.

Arabella

What shall we say to him?

Lucy

What role to play?

Tuneless

I don't know at all.

(Enter Bramble.)

Bramble

Listen, what's this all about? Vainly do I question everybody. Each one turns his back on me, without any response. Everyone in mourning. Nephew, why are you dressed in mourning?

Desmond (bowing and exiting)

Sir—

Bramble

Another fleeing mute. And you, Arabella, what have you to tell me?

Arabella (curtsying)

Not a thing, sir.

(Exit Arabella.)

Bramble

Again—hey, I beg you, Lucy, ease me of my uncertainty. Why the mourning?

Lucy

For a costume party.

(Exit Lucy.)

Bramble

And you, Tuneless—won't you explain to me what I already begin to suspect. If it were the Countess who was dead, then everybody would be in mourning—right? My dear Tuneless, hide nothing from me. You are my only confidant—

Tuneless

Well, but— (aside) What the devil am I going to say?

Bramble

What ought I to think in seeing all this?

Tuneless

In seeing all this black clothing, you ought to think they are dressed in black.

Bramble

Hmm! I doubt—

Tuneless

Tell me. What are you worried about? I will tell you if it is true.

Bramble

It must be, but I don't believe it.

Tuneless

Nor I, sir.

Bramble

My heart tells me enough. (hands over his eyes) My wife is dead.

Tuneless (aside)

This gives me an idea. Let him believe it. He is in love with Arabella, that's good, too. (aloud) Yes, my word, sir. There's no keeping it from you. One divines immediately what one fears or wishes most. You've guessed it. Your wife is—dead.

Bramble

I've observed that no one dared tell me the news.

Tuneless

It jumps right at you. I dared not tell you. I am certain you are strong enough to bear it.

Bramble

It happens to everybody.

Tuneless

You take it like a Caesar.

Bramble

I bet she died Saturday night.

Tuneless

Right.

Bramble

'Cause I woke from a dream with a terrible start.

Tuneless

You see the sympathy between those two who love each other.

Bramble

I sensed a cold hand.

Tuneless

And, she told you goodbye.

Bramble

I saw an invisible phantom there—who disappeared. But, how did her death occur?

Tuneless

I am going to tell you, sir. You know that Saturday night—

Bramble

Yes?

Tuneless

In the moment she appeared to you—death took her. But the ghost already told you—

Bramble

What happened?

Tuneless

Death took her. I don't like to tell sad tales like these.

Bramble

Tell me some circumstances.

Tuneless

If you absolutely wish to know the circumstances, I'll tell you right away that she died suddenly.

Bramble

Of apoplexy?

Tuneless

No, sir—of—of emotion. They just told her you had died at the wells. Suddenly, a seizure came on—and the faint turned into a coma—and you are now a widower.

Bramble (drawing out a handkerchief)

If it is true she died of sadness, I am obligated to weep. (low) But, how shall I manage it? Boo hoo.

Tuneless

Don't weep any more. I've got important business to discuss.

Bramble

Really, I've suffered an irreparable loss.

Tuneless

That can be repaired, sir—for—

Bramble

She was the best of wives—boo hoo.

Tuneless

Listen to me, please—

Bramble

Easy going—affectionate—boo hoo.

Tuneless

Listen, will you!

Bramble

Tender—boo—sincere—hoo—honest—boo—the best heart—the best heart—hoo—hoo—hoo.

Tuneless (aside)

If he's going to weep forever, he'll mess up my plans. (pulling Bramble by the arm) Sir, you make me feel compassion for you. The woman didn't die of sadness. I told you at first to console you. But the truth is—as all the doctors agree—she died of pure joy!

Bramble

I cannot believe she wished my death.

Tuneless

To wish your death, no, but she hoped you wouldn't live as long as she.

Bramble

Oh, as to that, I believe it, indeed.

Tuneless

She wished to inherit your wealth.

Bramble

Ah! Self-interest.

Tuneless

Interest rendered her soft and caressing. But, at the bottom she had a hardness for you.

Bramble

Ah, that's a bad heart.

Tuneless

You remember, one day, enraged against you, she had such self-control she was able to embrace you. She almost split. She told her maids all the injuries she wished, but didn't dare to express to you. In her mind, she was strangling you.

      Bramble

A bad woman.

      Tuneless

Malicious.

      Bramble

Secretive.

      Tuneless

Darkly so.

      Bramble

If I were so indignant—

      Tuneless

Malign—

      Bramble

Outrageous.

      Tuneless

Demonic.

Bramble

So extravagant.

Tuneless

She was a devil.

Bramble

If she hadn't died, I would kill her.

Tuneless

Therefore, cry no more. Recollect the tenderness you have for Arabella—remember you told me of it? In confidence, of course. If you still love that little Arabella, I warn you, the Countess intends to marry her today.

Bramble

Today!

Tuneless

From friendship, that's what I wish you to prevent. But, before going into that, it's essential that you avoid the Countess until we have taken certain measures with Arabella. But, hide yourself quickly in these apartments while I go to Arabella.

Bramble

You upset me.

Tuneless

Go in, quickly. (pushing him out) Because I will lead Arabella to you instantly.

(Exit Bramble.)

Tuneless

My idea is good; he's fallen into the trap. A weak little genius wrapped up in his business affairs—and stupid in everything else. One sees many like that. Now to prevent— But, if someone should undeceive him—(going, then stopping) Still, I have to go. (returning) Better stay. How to begin—

(Enter Mr. MacPherson and Mrs. MacPherson.)

Mrs. MacPherson

Ah, sir. Mr. Bramble is returned. What a misfortune!

MacPherson

He came posthaste. That's the trouble.

Mrs. MacPherson

There's the trouble.

MacPherson

If his wife sees him, she'll know he's not dead.

Mrs. MacPherson

No more marriage.

MacPherson

No partying—no wedding.

Mrs. MacPherson

No drinking.

MacPherson

Nothing.

Tuneless

Listen to me—if you want to celebrate, we must make him believe his wife is dead.

MacPherson

Ho, ho, ho—both dead.

Mrs. MacPherson

And both widows.

Tuneless

If he asks you—say no more than, "She is dead."—But when? But how? But why?

MacPherson

She is dead.

Tuneless

Very good. But that's not the only thing. We must prevent these two from meeting, and to do that you may have to counterfeit drunkenness.

Mrs. MacPherson

I'll take care of that. We will drink despite him.

Tuneless

Yes. Watch him for me until I come back.

(Exit Tuneless.)

MacPherson

We have to say, "Your wife is dead, and we're drinking

our sorrows."

Mrs. MacPherson

Maybe he can hear us. Sing something about his dead wife.

MacPherson

That's a fine idea. A fine idea. Hem, la, la, la. My wife is dead, my wife is dead, And my heart, it feels like lead— Ooh!

(Enter Bramble.)

Bramble

What's this? Do you rejoice in my sorrow?

MacPherson

Your wife is dead and we're drinking.

Mrs. MacPherson

And we are drinking.

Bramble

These rogues are drunk. (trying to leave)

MacPherson (stopping him)

Drink away your sorrows. It's the only way.

Bramble (trying to pass)

What's all this?

Mr. and Mrs. MacPherson

Console yourself. Sit down in this chair.

Bramble (forced to sit)

The devil!

Mrs. MacPherson

You wife has left us. It's sad. We must drink until she returns.

MacPherson

If my wife dies, I will get drunk for her epitaph.

Bramble

I'm getting nothing from these drunks. I'd better wait till Tuneless returns.

Mrs. MacPherson

While we're waiting for Tuneless, we'll sing you a little

song to chase your sorrows away.

Bramble

Death.

Mr. and Mrs. MacPherson

Heigh ho, heigh ho, it's off to the funeral we'll go, heigh ho, heigh ho—

(Enter Tuneless and Arabella.)

Tuneless

Silence. Get out. There, Miss, come on in.

(Exit Mr. and Mrs. MacPherson.)

Arabella

Here he is. I'm going to play my part wonderfully.

Bramble

Ah—they're gone. Let's join Tuneless.

Arabella

I come to ask your bounty, sir. I am desolate.

Bramble

Console yourself, my dear child. I will prevent the Countess from marrying you.

Arabella

She wants to marry me to a man with no money at all. That's what distresses me.

Tuneless

No money at all. Sir, you know she has nothing. And, when one marries without money—it makes for a lot of sad children. The Countess said this fellow had a fortune.

Arabella

I don't believe in fortunes, except when I see them already in existence.

Tuneless

She said he is young.

Arabella

Then, he will be unfaithful.

Tuneless

The older a man is, the more likely you'll love him for the rest of his life.

Arabella

I always wanted a husband with a settled disposition.

Tuneless

Who has been previously married.

Arabella

Who always indulges his wife in a thousand ways.

Tuneless

Like you, for example.

Arabella

Unfortunately, I will never be as happy as my aunt was.

Bramble

I like the prudence, the wisdom, and the good taste of this tasty little person.

Arabella

It's my natural taste, you know, sir. I am incapable of

loving a young man. But, I am capable of a real affection for those who treat me right.

Bramble

Noble sentiments, noble sentiments. I am so charmed, so delighted, that I am going to see the Countess right now. Ah, there she is in the gallery. I am going to speak to her this moment.

(Exit Bramble.)

Arabella

It's not going badly. But, if my aunt should come in—

Tuneless

Fear nothing. These two departed will not meet so soon. For Desmond is keeping the widow in the garden, and we are keeping the husband here. The Countess is in on the plot, and is going to keep him in his apartment, one way or another.

Arabella

Hurry then, to do on our side as well as Desmond has done on his.

Tuneless

You must make your contribution by making the old

widower in love, while Desmond does the same with the widow.

(Enter Steward, Countess, Lucy.)

Countess

Love doesn't hide itself, sir, and you have accosted me in a manner that convinces me you have a great deal for Arabella.

Bramble

Not at all, Madame, but with respect—

Countess

I have only one word to say to you about the matter. If you don't want me to marry off Arabella, and to keep her to console you in your grief, and then later marry her—then you must do something for your nephew. You know how highly I think of Desmond. I have spoken to you a hundred times for him—uselessly. And I am going to take this opportunity—the solicitor is downstairs—I am going to marry Arabella, before your very eyes, if you don't transfer some of your wealth to Desmond.

Bramble

I am a reasonable man.

Countess

We'll go see. But, come to my apartment to agree on the contract. Follow us, Arabella. Your presence will facilitate this little accommodation.

(Exit Bramble, Countess, Arabella, and Tuneless. After a moment, enter Desmond and Lucy.)

Desmond

Well, Lucy?

Lucy

They are about to tax your uncle. What have you done to hasten the liberality of our widow?

Desmond

I pressed her in a lively way. But she was pressing me in a lively way, also.

Lucy

Her love presses.

Desmond

I pretend not to understand her passionate talk. But the less I seem to understand, the more she reveals. I can't hold her back. I had to leave her alone in the garden—where she stayed to hide her confusion. She sighs, she excites herself—

Lucy

A declaration is coming. It wants to come forth. She will unburden her heart. She is meditating some passionate declaration which may be obscure—or plain enough.

Desmond

All too plain, I fear. I see her coming. I am not going to wait to hear this.

(Exit Desmond.)

Widow (entering)

Where did he go, Lucy?

Lucy (pointing her in the wrong direction)

That way, I think.

Widow

Desmond. Desmond. I must talk to you.

(Exit Widow. Enter Tuneless.)

Lucy

Ah, Tuneless, everything's a mess here.

Tuneless

Ah, Lucy, everything's even worse on the other side.

Lucy

Truly, she really wants to make a gift.

Tuneless

In truth, he wants to make a gift.

Lucy

But, Tuneless—

Tuneless

But, Lucy—

Lucy

But first, she wants to assure herself that Desmond—

Tuneless

He wishes to be first secure of Arabella. He will give, when the contract is signed.

Lucy

In signing the contract, she says.

Tuneless

I can't see any hope.

Lucy

My genius is exhausted.

Tuneless

Our intrigue falls of its own weight.

Lucy

She's too sly.

Tuneless

He's too clever. Very well. Lucy, let us at least have the pleasure of dashing their hopes of this double marriage.

Lucy

What you suggest will do no good as far as I can see. I haven't the audacity to laugh about it. They'll be furious.

(Exit Lucy.)

Tuneless

Me, I always have the courage to amuse myself. Let's see what will become of this. The husband is left alone in his apartment—his wife is alone in hers. They are both saddled for the race. Let's see who will win. Good, here's the husband. I also see the wife. Let's turn out the lights so as to make this double widowhood last a bit longer.

(Tuneless turns out the lights. Bramble enters.)

Bramble

The Countess thinks she's found her dupe. She intends to get me to give my money to Desmond, and then marry Arabella to whoever she pleases. But Arabella would be in despair not to marry me. I told her to meet me here so we could take some precautions. She's on her way. Let's wait here. (stepping into the shadows)

(Enter Widow.)

Widow

I can't find Desmond anywhere. Someone turned out the lights. He couldn't have given Arabella a rendez-vous here?

Bramble (aside)

If Arabella agrees, I will marry her, in spite of the

Countess. I've only to take her away secretly. But, what's happening?

Widow

It's Desmond, waiting for Arabella!

Bramble

Arabella is following me. How lucky I am, that she's promised to marry me. Ah!

Widow

How he sighs for her. The little traitor!

Bramble

It's Arabella who's looking for me. Here I am.

Widow

The resemblance of their voices always astonishes me. How I love one and hate the other.

Bramble

Am I the one you're looking for?

Widow

His voice makes me tremble— But, I am crazy—it's

Desmond's voice that sounds like that. I'll pretend to be Arabella. I've come to our rendezvous, my dear Desmond.

Bramble

Desmond—what, is it Desmond you come to see, after having promised never to be with anyone but me?

Widow

Ah! It's the true raging voice of my husband.

Bramble

Ingrate! Liar!

Widow

His ghost reproaches me.

Bramble

To betray me thus.

Widow

His ghost returns. Let's get out of here! (runs and falls into a chair) My legs have betrayed me! Let me call for help. Ah! My voice fails me.

Bramble

You wish to marry Desmond?

Widow

I didn't say that.

Bramble

What! Didn't I hear right— "Isn't it Desmond?"

Widow

Oh, no. I will never have another except you.

Bramble

Bah! Never have another—

Widow

No, no, husband, no.

Bramble

She trembles and calls me her husband. She fears the Countess. There's only me here—don't be afraid. Follow me.

Widow

Ha—a, a, a—

Bramble (taking her hand)

Where are you then?

Widow (fainting)

Ah.

Bramble

Don't be afraid—it's me who's got your hand.

Widow

I know it's you.

Bramble

Yes—while you call me your husband, you will be my wife. You will love me a little—right? Hey—modesty renders her silent. Hmm. How much more delightful this hand is to kiss than that of my late wife. Hers was rough, this is soft. But don't lose any time. Come with me. (pulling her) What is it? What's wrong?

Widow

Ah, Desmond—

Bramble

What do I hear?

(Enter Tuneless with a candle. The Widow and Bramble see each other, scream, and exit in different directions.)

Tuneless

I turn the thing into raillery. Now, we shall see. I have an idea that I must communicate to Lucy.

(Exit Tuneless.)

CURTAIN

ACT III

The lights darken, indicating the passage of time. Enter Arabella and Lucy.

Lucy

Mr. Bramble is outraged not to be a widower. He curses the Countess who has given him his false joy—but, he doesn't break with Tuneless, because he's afraid Tuneless will inform his dear lady of his infidelity. He still loves you, but he's still more amorous of inheriting from his wife. This should make it easier for Tuneless to bring him round.

Arabella

Really, what good can all this do?

Lucy

It may help—with luck. But frankly, I don't think it will help. Let's retire. I'm going to see in what shape my lady is in.

(Exit Lucy and Arabella. Enter Tuneless and Bramble.)

Tuneless

Yes, sir, it's dissimulation that keeps society going between men—civil and matrimonial.

Bramble

Ouf!

Tuneless

Under the shelter of dissimulation, courtiers embrace each other, women compliment each other, and authors bow to each other at a distance. Dissimulation creates new friendships and smoothes over old hatreds.

Bramble

Ouf!

Tuneless

Without dissimulation, how many secret separations would grow into public divorces. But dissimulation gives wisdom to men, joy to husbands—that's why there are so many happy families at present.

Bramble

Ah, my dear Tuneless—

Tuneless

You begin to dissimulate—. You hide from me your fear that I might reveal to your wife your passion for— Don't worry, I am discreet, and she herself cannot prove, even if she suspects, that you took her for Arabella—for you spoke low and she fainted.

Bramble

I am furious when I think—

Tuneless

That she didn't faint?

Bramble

The liar.

Tuneless

It's with lying that you find the way to dissimulate.

Bramble

What! All the caresses that she gave me for ten years were only to have my wealth.

Tuneless

While you permitted her to caress, so you could have

hers.

Bramble

A woman who hopes to outlive her husband is very unnatural.

Tuneless

For a man to wish to live longer than is wife is very—natural.

Bramble

To have a criminal passion for my nephew.

Tuneless

While you have an innocent tenderness for her niece.

Bramble

Heaven will punish her and all those who wish the death of others. Such people always die first.

Tuneless

Good. You will both predecease the other.

Bramble

Now, I must dissimulate to keep the peace at home,

and to preserve my honor before the world.

Tuneless

Very good. But, remember the essential thing. Send your nephew to the Indies.

Bramble

To the Indies. I will spare nothing to get him there.

Tuneless

Here—begin your dissimulation with the Countess. Go joke with her about the trick she played on you, and joke in the faces of all those who do nothing but laugh behind your back.

Bramble

That's the role I've got to take.

(Exit Bramble. After a moment, enter Lucy from another direction.)

Lucy

Well, Tuneless?

Tuneless

I've brought him to the point at which I want him. He

will dissimulate. But, I had trouble calming his rage.

Lucy

The rage of my mistress is very violent. To soften it, she fainted twice.

Tuneless

It's the strength of women to have such little weaknesses ready at their command. For when these great accidents occur—the attack is very strong—a woman saves herself by fainting or weeping.

Lucy

She fortifies herself in this way against reflections, and when she gets her strength back, there are tirades of abuse against her husband—but she leaves the name blank.

Tuneless

Let's finish. It's time to manage the interview.

Lucy

Yes. Here's the lady—bring on the husband.

Tuneless

I'll go fetch him.

(Exit Tuneless. Enter Widow from another direction.)

Widow

Where are you at, Lucy? You've abandoned me in my rage. I am furious against the Countess.

Lucy

That is to say, against your husband.

Widow

To deceive me, to betray me. He wanted me to die—the cruel man—the traitor.

Lucy

Oh, yes, more a traitor than the Countess. But, your husband also deserves your rage. First of all, because he is alive—and because he is unfaithful. But for fear that he may realize you are also unfaithful, feign, Madame, as I have told you.

Widow

I tremble with fear that he suspects me. Perhaps, in my mourning, I innocently called on Desmond.

Lucy

Innocently, of course. But now virtue and propriety

insist, that in the batting of an eye, you change your love into esteem. And, if your husband should eventually die, you may, in another bat of an eye, change your esteem into love.

Widow

Your advice is so wise. I will follow it. And send Arabella a hundred leagues from here.

Lucy

So. Let's go, and embrace your husband as if nothing happened.

Widow

It will be very hard to hide my anger.

(Enter Tuneless and Bramble.)

Lucy

Here he is. Recall all the feelings you had on your wedding day.

Widow

I do. I'm freezing. My blood is like ice.

Lucy

It's conjugal tenderness thawing.

Tuneless

Force yourself. Let no rancor show on your face.

Lucy

Courage, Madame.

Tuneless

Make an effort, sir.

Lucy

Strength.

Tuneless

Go on, now.

(Bramble and the Widow look at each other and run to embrace. As they hug, their faces show outraged grimaces.)

Bramble

I see my dear wife again.

Widow

And my equally dear husband!

(They embrace and separate several times, breathing like divers who surface for air, nauseated.)

Bramble

Ecch!

Widow

Ouf!

Bramble (turning to his wife with a joyful, but somehow tortured, look)

My joy is so great that it's frightful—ah-ecch!

Widow

My delight is too much to bear—yuck!

Bramble

Why is it that your joy appears troubled?

Widow

Emotions of rage come over me—against the Countess. In making you believe I was dead, she exposed you to a possible seizure. You might have died.

Bramble

You?—she would've enjoyed to make me die.

Widow

Thank God's mercy, you look—well. You appear healthy. I am furious with—that woman.

Bramble

All this has merely redoubled my feelings for you. I can't really express them.

Widow

I feel, also, that my love for you—I don't know how to say it. Huh—how I hate the Countess.

Bramble

This is like a renewal of the feelings I had for you when we first met.

Widow

Yes. It's like a second honeymoon.

Tuneless

A posthumous marriage.

Bramble

A renewal of my love. Yes, I also wish to take these little precautions that will assure you are cared for properly when I die.

Widow

I want you to survive me to enjoy my wealth. All that you deserve of it.

Bramble

As, so as to no longer have to put up with the presence of anyone around me who might take something from you when I die, I've decided to send my nephew to the Indies.

Widow (with surprise and spite)

And, for the same reason, I—I am going to marry Arabella a hundred leagues from here.

Bramble

You tell me that with a little spite. It's innocently that I speak to you of separating from Desmond.

Widow

And, I have nothing but pure good intentions in separating from Arabella.

(Enter the Countess's Maid.)

Maid

Here is the Countess, coming to rejoice. We are going to sing and dance all night. It's not only for the three marriages I see on the agenda, WE are ready for a wedding, you see.

Bramble

What's that about three weddings?

Maid

Yours first—for the Countess regards all this as a new marriage.

Widow

She's right. But not one made in Heaven.

Bramble

And the two others?

Maid

Don't you know? Didn't you know the joke was to get money from you to marry Desmond in Wales. And you, Madame, understood, of course, that the money asked from you was to marry Arabella in Scotland. But, since you refused to give it, the Countess is bearing the expenses herself.

Widow (low, to Lucy)

Desmond in Wales!

Lucy

Keep a straight face—virtue.

Bramble

Arabella in Scotland!

Tuneless

Shut up, sir. Dissimulation.

(Enter the Countess, Arabella, Desmond, and the MacPhersons.)

Countess

I come to share your joy in being reunited, in seeing each other again, like Orpheus and Eurydice. And to celebrate the two marriages I've made. Now, enjoy yourselves.

(The MacPhersons start to sing: La, la, la—)

Countess

Stop the singing. I perceive that instead of rejoicing you, something saddens you. There's something here I don't understand. When I marry a nephew who displeases you so much that you are sending him away—

Bramble

Send him away, Madame, that's what I wish—

Countess

And, when I take your niece off your hands—

Widow

You please me greatly, Madame.

Countess

Arabella will leave tomorrow for Scotland.

Widow

I consent, but—

Countess

And your nephew to Wales—

Bramble

That's what I want—but—

Countess

Why then, are you both irritated, when I do what contents each of you?

Lucy

Madame doesn't want to be separated from her only niece.

Tuneless

The gentleman always wishes to see his dear nephew.

Countess

I don't believe that you love them at all. Yet—your tenderness for them gives me an idea. It would keep them here. I'll marry them to each other—if you give your consent to it.

Tuneless

This marriage would enrage your wife, and—Arabella

would always be where you could get at her.

Lucy

This marriage would punish your husband, and someday, with Desmond about, you might—

Countess

You hesitate at this second proposition. That makes me suspect—

Widow

Not at all, Madame.

Bramble

You deceive yourself.

Countess

What then made you stop?

Widow

Because, Madame, having destined my wealth for a husband who is unspeakably dear to me—

Bramble

Yes, Madame, and to protect mine for a loving spouse—

Countess

Oh, I'm delighted to be deceived in my suspicions. I see the point that causes you hesitation. I ask nothing for them. Leave your money to each other, and let them take from the survivor. That way, they will ultimately get all your wealth, and you will take proper care of your spouse.

Desmond (to Widow)

Madame, prevent them from separating me from your presence.

Arabella (to Bramble, low)

Sir, will you let them take me away from you into Scotland?

Bramble

What determines me is the fear of—of displeasing my wife.

Widow

The fear that I have of angering my husband—

Countess

Then, the marriage is made. Give your hands.

Tuneless

Such a pretty marriage merits a complete opera. But unfortunately, we have neither musicians nor dancers. And, in the town they have only peasants. Be content, therefore, to listen to the little cantata I have composed. We are going to rehearse it in your presence. And, while we lack musicians, I myself will sing it for you. La, la, la.

(While Tuneless is getting ready, they all run away.)

CURTAIN

ABOUT THE TRANSLATOR

Frank J. Morlock has written and translated many plays since retiring from the legal profession in 1992. His translations have also appeared on Project Gutenberg, the Alexandre Dumas Père web page, Literature in the Age of Napoléon, Infinite Artistries. com, and Munsey's (formerly Blackmask). In 2006 he received an award from the North American Jules Verne Society for his translations of Verne's plays. He lives and works in México.

www.ingramcontent.com/pod-product-compliance
Lightning Source LLC
LaVergne TN
LVHW041623070426
835507LV00008B/427